THE LIES WE WERE TOLD

From Foehood to Sisterhood

Dr. Eloise M. Fulton-Taylor

ARCHWAY
PUBLISHING

Archway Publishing books may be ordered through booksellers or by contacting:

Archway Publishing
1663 Liberty Drive
Bloomington, IN 47403
www.archwaypublishing.com
1 (888) 242-5904

AU pic credit: Sarita Garlic a photographer with Photo Illusions

ISBN: 978-1-4808-8019-1 (sc)
ISBN: 978-1-4808-7728-3 (hc)
ISBN: 978-1-4808-8020-7 (e)

Library of Congress Control Number: 2019909892

Print information available on the last page.

Archway Publishing rev. date: 08/12/2019

To all the women (and girls) who've ever wondered why our relationships are strained. To every woman (and girl) who knows that it's time for the lies about us and the lies we believe about one another to stop. To everyone who's ever believed that things can get better if only we have an opening opportunity for change. To all the groundbreaking leaders of society: women (and girl) entrepreneurs who know what it takes to pioneer change. Finally, to my mother, who taught me my worth when I felt devalued by my own difference. It was this difference that allowed the Lord to write His plan for us through me as outlined in these pages. Please know that conflict, contention, and strained relationships were not created by us but created for us. However, if we keep holding on to them through our beliefs, values, and actions we're surrendering to their control over us instead of taking control over them and establishing a new form of engagement between us. So if you're holding this book in your hand and want to move from the lies to the truth, from foehood to sisterhood, then don't put it back on the shelf, because this book is for you. Together, let's embrace the leadership of sisterhood!

Contents

Foreword

Relationships between men and women are in trouble. In today's society, women still appear to be in survival mode. From childhood to adulthood, from the past to modern day, patriarchy's negative impact rages on. Oh, the backlash this creates in male/female relationships! The anxiety it causes in the spirit of some women who can't quite put their finger on what is wrong! It's truly overwhelming. *The Lies We Were Told: From Foehood to Sisterhood* is Dr. Taylor's journey back to the basics to examine the system of patriarchy in our society that has left women feeling devalued and powerless.

Through biblical insights, Taylor examines God's original design for women. As creation longs for the original plan of peaceful coexistence, the groans of weary women have come before the throne of God. The system of patriarchy has caused many women to interact in negative ways with one another. As women, we must disconnect from the patriarchal myths that have damaged us and reconnect with one another. This book offers a new vision and fresh insight that reveals the truth about how a woman can learn how to fulfill God's plan to lead with confidence and grace in every area of endeavor—work, home, family, friendship, relationships, and spiritual growth.

It is true that patriarchy can only flourish in an unhealthy, ungodly environment. So it is the responsibility of every woman who feels the impact of such an ungodly system to change the narrative. Dr. Taylor boldly and courageously examines the myths that have affected every generation for thousands of years and are still at work in society today. As we cling to the truth from God's Word that tells us we are "fearfully and wonderfully made," let the revelation of what that truly means saturate our being, releasing us to celebrate womanhood and to rejoice in the gift that we are to the world.

May the following pages stir in your spirit the inspiration, motivation, and passion to "thrive and survive" and truly recover and be restored from "the lies we were told."

Dr. Millicent Hunter
Senior Pastor, the Baptist Worship Center Church

Introduction

The DNA of foehood first appeared more than 1000 years ago. It is an acid that has eaten away at the civility of society. It has eaten away at interactions and verbal exchanges between males and females. The destructive acid of foehood has also eaten away at us by fostering and promoting a false sense of togetherness on a large scale. And specifically, it has helped in fostering and promoting a false sense of sisterhood. This false sense of sisterhood, for centuries, has welcomed our Dysfunctional/ Damaging Negative Actions. What we didn't know was that our actions coded in its DNA were not a real reflection of us: our true selves, but a mirror image of what a male dominated society wants us to be. Foes.

The number one cause of contentious relationships in society is *patriarchy*. It's a system that puts men at the head of the family and defines how women relate to one another, how men and women engage, and social responsibilities for women as leaders.

In the interest of survival, patriarchy has created an invisible but powerful negative effect that some consider correct and just. But it denies the rights of half the human population based on a system that promotes men's pleasure and dominance.

With cultural support from one generation to the next, patriarchy has managed to thrive. It defines our social relationships, including friendship, marriage, and family.

The influence of patriarchy has affected every generation for thousands of years, and it's at work in society today. It is not bound or limited by nationality, race, religion, or creed, and it crosses geographic borders as well. Patriarchy expresses itself as manipulation, dominance, control, and superiority. Known in present-day society as absolute male dominance, its real name is patriarchy. It is patriarchy that created gender defining and identifying pronouns for God and automatically assigned only a male gender, when both male and female were created in the image of God. Patriarchy has impacted greatly the strained relationships between men and women; boys and girls. Even its values, beliefs, and actions have touched male female relationships in all of society. Business and commerce has been touched by it and how men and women are treated there has been affected. Social, political, and civic arenas have been infected by its ravaging DNA. And religious organizations as well as educational institutions have felt the strained effects borrowed from its tainted disposition. Yes, patriarchy is the root cause, or at least one of the main root causes, of relationship breakdowns. In subsequent books I will delve more deeply into its impact on other of society's playgrounds. But in this book I will only address how the stain of patriarchy has affected, impacted, and eaten away at us-women, girls, and our sisterhood.

Please understand that patriarchy can only flourish in unhealthy environments. So it's up to those who feel its impact most—women—to change the narrative. With its lies, patriarchy has shaped and informed our ideas about ourselves and one another, creating hostility and abuse. With this book, I'm sending out a clarion call to all women. It's time to wake up to the origin of certain behaviors among us. I'm also calling on all women to help change the story created about us but not by us. Our choices and our voices have long been denied and silenced, and that forced us to internalize patriarchy's lies for centuries.

I have often wondered why women seem conditioned to naturally distrust one another. We were told by society and perhaps by personal experience the following:

1. Women can't offer genuine support.
2. Women can't be true friends to one another outside of a clique.
3. Jealousy is rampant among women, and it governs how we treat one another.

4. Women can't stand to see other women have more than they have.
5. If a woman isn't in the limelight and being celebrated, she can't and won't applaud your success without slipping in some criticism.
6. Women can't be trusted with our partners because, given the opportunity, they can't pass up a chance to stab us in the back and steal them from us.
7. Women are always criticizing and judging one another harshly.

But why are we so critical of one another? Why do we judge one another's looks, decisions, circumstances, and families? Growing up I was told that conflict among women (and girls) was common. Growing up I was told that harsh criticism among us should be expected and accepted. But most importantly, growing up, I could never get a clear answer why. All I heard was "That's just how women are" or "You know how women are." These dismissive answers made me tired, upset, and very concerned. For me, they represented a mantra that the world seems to accept as the female norm. But what if I told you the following:

1. Women are capable of genuine support.
2. We are more than capable of true friendship.
3. We aren't jealous of one another.
4. We really can celebrate one another's accomplishments.

5. We are honored to be part of your winner's circle.
6. We aren't on the lookout for a chance to stab you in the back or sleep with your partner.
7. We can speak well of one another.

Would you believe me? What if I told you that the girlfriend who stabbed you in the back wasn't really stabbing you in the back? She was really trying to trash the memory of her own devastating situation, and you just happened to be in the way. Could you believe that? Is it possible that the friend you just fell out with after thirty years of friendship wasn't really jealous of you at all? She was just trying to stabilize her own position in life. Was she really trying to hurt you, or was she trying to help herself become *more*?

And what if I told you that the bullying you faced as a child (or perhaps as an adult) by other females wasn't because you were insecure, conceited, confident, or arrogant. It was actually because those little girls, now grown-ups, were acting out of a cultural system used to control their actions. They never had a chance to understand how they were really supposed to act. In fact, the unhealthy environment created by patriarchy conditioned women to act like bullies.

If you knew this to be true, could you find it in your heart and mind to believe me? Could you feel sympathy for the women who helped make your life miserable from childhood to adulthood? Well, in this book, I'm telling you just that! I'm telling you that the stage was set long ago for the conflict between you and other women.

This book will challenge us to see one another differently. It offers a new vision that sees women against the backdrop of a well-established but faulty system meant to control us. Patriarchy linked women's stability to toxic systems of forced competition, hierarchy, and survival challenges. I'm proposing that instead of seeing one another as rivals who are only out for revenge and punishment, we see each other as by-products of someone else's idea.

This book will challenge us to see the harm done to us and by us to one of our sisters as something influenced by an invisible system, not the result of spite. The historical and cultural conditioning that is patriarchy was established well before you and I were born. Before our mothers and their mothers and even their mothers were born, this system existed.

Patriarchy is responsible for entrapping our minds and convincing the world that women can't get along and never will. It has controlled women's environments for thousands of years. Instead of harmony, instead of trusting one another and treating one another according to godly principles, it has kept us from being seen and acting as God intended for us to be seen and to act. The following pages will unpack and explain the lies we were told and their impact on our current relationships.

Chapter 1

On the Playground

When I was a little girl, the playground was an important social gathering place. Friendships were made, enemies were identified, and insecurities were definitely felt. More often than not, if you didn't fit into a certain mold defined by the community, you were left out of the larger group. You may have been picked on or passed over, but most traumatically, you ran home because of what did or didn't happen on the playground.

So what made us cry the most? Was it the boys who pulled our hair, teased us, or tried to kiss us? Or was it our social experiences with other girls who, like us, desperately wanted to survive another day on the playground? I think it was the latter.

On the playground, survival was my primary goal. Back then, I could not have put into words exactly what it was that had to survive. But today when I look back on my playground experiences, I have come to understand that the *I* who needed to survive was *me*, the total me: my self-esteem, my confidence, and my self-worth. I had to be part of a clique in order to keep my self-esteem—if I had any—intact. This was an unspoken requirement on the playground of my childhood.

There's nothing wrong with having a circle of friends, but it sometimes became vicious when the circle dealt harshly with outsiders. The law of the playground jungle was that if you had to treat others harshly in order to protect your self-esteem, your confidence, and your physical self, then that's what you did. And if survival meant you had to become a bully or be loyal to one, you gave in and joined the clique in order to get along and stay alive. If you had to criticize or laugh or jeer, especially at other girls, then you did.

In most, if not all, cultures and communities, every girl on the playground engaged in these behaviors. It didn't matter whether your family was affluent, middle class, or lower income. When it came to female survival, the rules of the playground were the same. This behavior was culturally acceptable and seen as normal for girls.

What we didn't know was that this behavior played right into the hands of patriarchy's established portrayal of females. We were mirroring behaviors of the past, when women fought to survive more than a millennium ago. Like us, they needed to protect their self-esteem, confidence, and self-worth. Before I delve into how patriarchy conditioned women to interact long ago, let me transport us from the playground to adulthood.

What I remember vividly about the playground is that as a child I was heavily influenced by others. It wasn't just what my mother or father or family may have taught me about being proud of myself. But what others also thought about me that shaped my confidence, self-esteem, and self-worth. This in turn informed my transition into adulthood and how I interacted and behaved as an adult engaging with others, especially other women. The social skills I learned as a little girl on the playground went on to dictate my behavior as an adult.

The proverbial adult playground on which female survival is challenged includes professional settings, such as work-places and networking events. It also includes civic, social and religious organizations, such as schools and the church.

Playgrounds past and present in childhood and adult-hood have one thing in common when it comes to girls and women, boys and men: we're made to feel that survival is our top priority. When we feel threatened in any way, we respond with familiar behavior. We employ the tools of fear, force, abuse, disregard, adverse competition, rivalry and so on. These are the tools we were told was okay and ac-ceptable to have in our survival arsenal and use at will. For centuries, the ways of patriarchy have been familiar. Good or bad, right or wrong, nice or nasty, survival challenges bring out an animal instinct for doing what's deemed essential to survive.

Patriarchy's Invisible Impact on the Playground

Patriarchy refers to extreme social dominance by men. It means that men's authority and thinking control every aspect of society. Historically, women, children, and entire families depended on the male head of the household. They behaved according to the desires of men in order to survive. In short, women's survival was determined by the male leader of the family.

Under patriarchy, if a woman survived poverty, childlessness, or the death of a male family member, it usually meant that somehow she found favor with a man in the family. All we have to do is look to the biblical story of Ruth (Boaz) and Naomi. So women had to make themselves pleasing to men—desirable, desiring, and humble.

If a woman's words and actions didn't agree with the man's, her true voice was silenced. She had to be pleasing or risk being replaced through murder, divorce, or demotion to a lower position among the other women in the family or family system. If a man didn't have a strong desire for a woman, her stability would be in constant jeopardy. Women had to present themselves as less in both dignity and importance compared to men.

Dominated by men and their rules, women were forced to compete with one another for men's desire. If a man fancied one particular woman over another, the survival of the least favored was seen as threatened. This system of forced competition among women not only threatened their survival but also created a permanent atmosphere of distrust.

More than a thousand years ago, patriarchy forced women into competition with one another because, under this system, men were socially and legally entitled to have many women at once. The household included not just one woman but many. Because women's value (and therefore survival) was based on their ability to have children—especially sons—they all wanted to bear the head of the household's offspring. So at any given time a household had one man, hundreds of women who were either wives or concubines, and many children. Today we might call this a blended family, full of half brothers and sisters.

A woman's status as a wife or concubine and her possession of property and wealth played an immense role in how she was positioned or categorized. If she came from a wealthy family with property and was given in marriage, she was usually assigned the role of wife. A woman from a poor family of limited means who was given in marriage was placed in the position of slave, servant, or concubine.

Women from poor families could be bought and sold into a harem, where they were not wives but concubines or sex servants. In other words, they were not wife material.

In today's culture, we'd say she was *wifey* material. *Wifey* in today's culture means *side chick*, *booty-call girl*, *friend with benefits*, *baby mama*, and so on.

Women from wealthy families were given more care and prestige even though they were still considered property. When given in marriage, they had the upper-class role of wife. Wives were treated with greater respect and given more authority over the other women, as well as the welfare of the children in the household. In contrast, concubines were seen as lowly servants to both men and their wives (women of higher position).

This family structure dynamic encouraged female discord at the survival level. If a wife's position was challenged by a concubine, the two could come to blows. Even at this time in history, women on the so-called adult playground were desperate to protect their confidence, self-esteem, and self-worth. And when women are forced to navigate a ranked order of relationships, they ultimately do what is necessary to survive.

Women faced other survival challenges on the historical playground of patriarchy. For example, in times of war, men went off to defend and maintain the family's livelihood and wealth. If the head of the household was killed, his family was left without an appointed leader and the necessary protections to continue the family.

At such times, women's survival instincts were heightened because both wives and concubines wanted their sons to be chosen as the next leader. They had a chance to be elevated by a son who took over the father's position, and their status secured. The result was female rivalry.

Another source of rampant female rivalry involved envy of others' positions, power, and leadership. Violent actions often took place. Some women poisoned other women, and some children killed other children. Historically, the fight for survival pitted wives against concubines or other wives, brothers against brothers, and sisters against sisters. All of this led to household chaos and created specific mind-sets about survival.

These episodes shaped and informed certain survival mind-sets within us. These survival mind-sets were initially the product of circumstance and *not* choice.

Please note that it was the unhealthy environment created by patriarchy that gave rise to the friction in women's relationships with one another and not something inherently female. I believe that if patriarchy hadn't created an environment of rivalry in which a woman's survival depended on how well she pleased the male leader, women wouldn't be inclined to behave in ways that sow discord between them even today.

In today's society, women still appear to be in survival mode. Surviving the impact of forced competition, whether professionally, socially, economically, or religiously. Surviving the difficulties of being impoverished. And surviving the disparities between male and female. From childhood to adulthood, from the past to modern day, patriarchy's impact rages on and causes the best of us to act in ways that reflect an obsolete mind-set. But it's time for a new vision that reveals the truth about how women's mind-sets evolved to seeing one another as enemies or foes. Beginning now our new actions will help us dispel the myths of patriarchy and the lies we've been told about women's ability to lead with confidence and grace.

Myths about Female Leadership

Men's dominance in society and women's duty to appease and please them set us up for discord by controlling our thoughts and actions. Deborah, Esther and even Queen Vashti are the exception, not the rule here but, more often than not, women weren't allowed to show their pure leadership abilities. Leaders write their own stories and take pride in reporting how they handled difficulties. But patriarchy hijacked our voices and wrote the story for us. And the story that was told was one-sided and only represented how men wanted or expected us to feel about our experiences. Not how we actually felt about our experiences. For example, Rachel and Leah. How did they really feel about being physically compared to one another? Were they hurt or embarrassed by how their father spoke of them? Did his words or treatment make them angry? And did Leah cry because of humiliation when she was by herself? Did Leah feel inferior and Rachel superior? Did Rachel take every opportunity to remind Leah of how *unattractive* she was? Were they able to protect each other from the gossip of how they were being labeled? There are so many more questions to be derived from this story. But we don't know the answers too many of them. What is known is that when our social interactions are connected to any kind of forced competition where we are compared to others, our worth is called into question. And when that happens, our need to exist takes priority and gives rise to a fight. It is this fight that confronts a mind-set and thought process that's already in place.

In the past when one woman treated another with insolence, it wasn't an altogether natural behavior. It was an instinctive response under the system of patriarchy that drove her to do whatever it took to survive. This by-any-means-necessary attitude was and is the controlling force behind patriarchy.

Women's task now is to take the lead role when it comes to female relationships and rewrite the rules. We must define for ourselves how women's interactions should look, rejecting all shadows from the past involving forced competition, status, and desperation to survive.

In truth, the reason women's relationships with one another haven't evolved in tandem with female leadership is that past conditioning and belief systems control our thoughts about one another. Our actions have been based on a narrative that grew out of an old power system that's dominated our survival instincts for years. If we want a new narrative to emerge from the ashes of conflict and contention, we must look beyond the definitions that have entrapped our thinking about the female norm.

The Old Narrative

Women have been at odds with one another for one reason and one reason only—because of patriarchy's lies. One of the biggest lies it told us was that unattached to people or things we have no value. When you're conditioned to believe that only a man can empower you to find your wealth, value, purpose, and stability in life, you begin to doubt your leadership abilities. Your ability to stand alone if necessary, and lead, because you are enough. We've never dealt with the underlying reasons for our hostile attitudes toward one another because historically it was unacceptable to do so.

The old story said we didn't mind being the other woman. It said we were okay with humiliating, hurting, or poisoning one another or our stepchildren for the sake of survival. The world didn't know we suffered in silence because we really didn't want our displeasure with this kind of existence to be known, as we protected the system heads, and it was the only one we were granted. But we've evolved and gained more control over our thinking, and more choices have become available to us. So the old narrative should no longer command our allegiance, because it's what shattered our confidence in ourselves and our abilities in the first place.

The old story of female rivalry portrayed women's inability to coexist within a family when two or more were tied to the same man. A drama played out when multiple sets of children of different mothers had the same father. It played out when resources for daily living and survival, however scarce, had to be shared. It played out when a woman wanted to lay with her husband but found him in the bed of another woman.

The story of how women felt about living under these conditions has never been told by women themselves. That's because patriarchy encouraged women to make men look good and sound good at any cost, even if they had to die trying. In patriarchy's narrative, women's voices were silent about how things really affected them emotionally and physically. And when feelings are suppressed instead of expressed, we often lash out in anger that's directed at other victims and not the perpetrators. Women's resentment and hostility were channeled toward one another instead of against the system of oppression.

An unhealthy environment can produce female leaders, but usually they show signs of being conditioned to react from a mind-set of systematic oppression. It's like an automatic response toward her sisters, whom she's not aware *are* her sisters. Thus, any stimuli from other women that make her feel uncomfortable connects with a pre-scripted message in her mind that *women are my enemies because they want what I have; they want my man, my resources, my opportunities, my benefits and blessings, and my status and position.*

At work or in social settings, in civic and professional organizations, or as part of religious institutions, the old narrative about women is still alive and with us. And society continues to accept it because the leadership by women that's necessary to dismantle the lies we were told hasn't existed. Now it's beginning.

Until now, we haven't looked to history for the answer to why female relationships have been so strained. But I became aware of the vicious fighting among women, both in the church and in society, despite our common struggles. I felt I'd discovered a real problem that only the emergence of female leadership could address. Our new narrative must begin with female leaders standing up and shouting to their sisters, "It wasn't you; it was a system I didn't even know existed that poisoned my attitude toward you. I apologize. Can you ever forgive me?"

What we did to one another and what was done to us on the playground, whether as children or adults, has to be addressed in order to clear the slate for a new narrative. In fact, what occurred on the playgrounds demands real action toward reconciliation for the future of our daughters, and their daughters too.

We can replace the old narrative with a new narrative of what sisterhood really looks like, freed from the toxic effects of patriarchy. Our new narrative must arise from a new attitude toward women. An attitude that believes, regardless of her status in life or her position in society, she is highly regarded, respected, and esteemed because of her life experiences that contribute to female connectedness and how we relate to one another.

The old narrative started with the premise that we are one another's enemies. The new narrative must start with, "You are not my enemy but my sister through experience." The old narrative said, "You want the same person I want" or "You did me dirty to get what I had." The old narrative said, "You want my position and will do whatever it takes to snatch it from me." The old narrative said, "You want the status or position that I worked hard for, but you just want it handed to you." The old narrative said, "You want my benefits and opportunities." And finally, the old narrative said, "If you have to kill me—my spirit, my reputation, and my confidence—to take me out so you can steal my position, so be it."

The new narrative must be created out of a clear understanding that God is in control. He blesses who He chooses to bless and moves in His own time, and when it's my turn, it will be His time. God will reward and bless me with the desires of my heart when He is ready to. The new narrative starts with a faith that says, "God has not forgotten about me. Therefore, I don't need to take what you have or hurt you in any way to survive in this life." In other words, a new narrative of sisterhood builds a healthy environment in place of what used to be.

With a new narrative on the playground there's no adverse competition for the same position or resources or benefits or power or profession because your faith is in God. Your confidence is derived from God and not from men. Not from titles. Not from status. And not from position.

Women and Hierarchy

A hierarchy is a system with different levels of rank or status. It allows leadership to develop and thrive but can create anxiety for those governed by the leader. This isn't surprising because we don't know what to expect or what influences the leader. The level of tension in any hierarchy depends on how the leader's thinking affects those who are impacted by it. If we feel threatened in any way, then our relationship with the leader is strained, especially when all the power is at the top and the rest of us have little or no say.

If a leader emerges from an unhealthy environment where power and authority were exercised by mistreating others, he or she tends to be abusive in order to feel in total control. Such leaders thrive only when they can dominate others. As long as the playing field *isn't* level, they feel secure. But they are extremely uncomfortable with the idea of anyone else being their equal in ideas, love, status, or position. For a leader or anyone in a position of power in an unhealthy environment, balance is uncomfortable. Imbalance is how they thrive.

A female leader who emerges from an unhealthy environment is under the influence of patriarchy's imbalances. Real balance represents a serious threat to her confidence, self-esteem, livelihood, and overall self-image. Therefore, adverse competition is always present in this type of scenario. Relationships in the workplace and elsewhere become strained when you must compete to stay where you are in an unhealthy environment. In an unhealthy environment, the competition is or can become vicious for those who lack a personal sense of security within themselves. Friends or allies can become "frienemies" and opponents. When we don't feel good about ourselves or feel insecure and threatened in any way we act out against one another. This applies to men and women; boys and girls.

A biblical example from the Old Testament is the relationship between Sarah and Hagar. Sarah was Abraham's wife, and Hagar was a servant and concubine who also served Sarah. When it appeared that God wasn't going to keep His promise to give Sarah and Abraham a child, Sarah offered to let Hagar bear Abraham's child. Hagar's son Ishmael was Abraham's firstborn. A bond formed between Hagar and Abraham that Sarah had no part in, a parental bond that created anger and jealousy in a competitive family system.

In biblical times (and often today), a woman's desire was for the happiness of her husband (or male leader). Hagar's rise from servant and concubine to mother of the firstborn child and the resulting bond between Hagar and Abraham changed the entire game. Hagar now had something over Sarah, something Sarah was not pleased about. Sarah wanted to conceive and, initially, couldn't, but Hagar could and did. Their relationship was strained in the first place because of the unhealthy environment of sharing a man which resulted in forced competition, and secondly because both women's status changed. Both were responsible for pleasing Abraham—bearing a child, but only one was able to do so. Sarah found herself in the position of having to compete for affection, and the two women were forced into rivalry. Both women were acting in response to the system which dictated their sole survival. Their sole survival was dependent upon successfully pleasing the system of patriarchy, the man.

A more modern example of how patriarchy creates unhealthy social environments that affect our relationships with our sisters, at times, are some of our modern day blended families. Beautiful innocent children, who are absolute blessings to the world, born into family systems where there is one young man (father) with multiple children by more than one mother. There are times when the mothers vie for the continued attention and affection from the father for their children or for themselves. In an unhealthy environment, these mothers and sometimes even their children are at war with one another. Physically, emotionally, and spiritually wounding one another. The only one who benefits, at least as is depicted more often than not, in the public arenas like celebrity status or the people in our own families and or communities, is the man. The man appears to be the one to have his choice of these young women at will. And the women begrudge one another repeatedly as they fight again and again over the young man (or men). Another example is with our sisters in the music industry. Today's pop music culture have very successful female artists. Newcomers, and those who have been in the industry much longer and has an established following. When new artist become a household name, it puts established artists in a position of struggle for professional survival. Her brand, her status at the top, and her artistry must survive.

The discord between at least four of these artist led to such viciousness that their behavior was plastered all over the news and social media. What made them act this way? I'll tell you what. It was the adversarial survival instinct created by patriarchy. All feel threatened by the forced competition. Its result is one artist pitted against another artist in sound, beauty, capability and so on.

It's been said that art imitates life, and we can see it in these stories. Sets of women who rises unexpectedly from low status to higher status could and does result in conflict. Emotionally, there was no winner in the story of Sarah and

Hagar, and no one is winning in the stories of these pop culture music industry artists.

Simply stated, our problem is not with one another. It's with this damned system of patriarchy that keeps causing us to react out of a dysfunctional storyline! As the tabloids reported, when these four artists became equal on certain levels, of success, vicious fighting resulted—emotional, psychological, verbal and perhaps even a little physical.

There's nothing wrong with hierarchy in and of itself. Whether between women or members of opposite sex, these types of relationships are part of life and necessary for commerce, leadership, servanthood, growth, and any type of business. But when hierarchy exists in an unhealthy environment, the lies of patriarchy excuse negative behavior in times of difficult change.

Sometimes negative behavior is justified, but sometimes it's just our response to a perceived threat to our confidence, self-esteem, and survival. This is usually a sign of patriarchy's influence. As children on the playground, our confidence depended on how others felt about us or made us feel about ourselves. We didn't operate on the basis of our own inner values. Our self-worth was derived from our connections to other people (including our families) and to things.

On the playground, if you had the latest fashions or the most up to date polished look, you felt like you were somebody. And guess what? Others felt like you were somebody too. However, if other females were also up to date in their looks and fashions, the toxicity of patriarchy kept us from seeing ourselves as special or important when the light of success or beauty shone brightly on someone else at the same time. It's as if we feared that our shine was somehow lessened by our sister's glow. We may feel diminished by another woman's importance, or as though we disappear, but we have to remind ourselves that this is a lie created by patriarchy to divide, conquer, and control us. This is the lie that says my beauty, power and authority is only credible or valid if it is compared to and evaluated against someone else. Or my shine is seen or brighter if shone against some-one or something that I or society considers less bright, by comparison.

Socially, we're so connected to the old narrative of pa-triarchy that we don't even realize it. As women, we must disconnect from it in order to reconnect with one another.

On the playground, if you were pretty or felt pretty or at least measured up to the current standards of pretty, you were drawn to other pretty girls. Your actions demonstrated the feelings you shared with others and about yourself, good or bad. If you were considered unattractive because of your looks, or if you felt ugly, you connected with other girls who felt the same way about themselves. Their behaviors became your behaviors. In short, dysfunctional friendships develop in unhealthy environments characterized by thinking that says my confidence depends on your insecurity. Or my beauty depends on your fitting into what true beauty has been defined to be.

Dysfunctional relationships between women exist today because we bought the story that says one woman's superior position depends upon another woman's inferior position. Or, I can't be top-notch if your success draws attention away from me. Unhealthy environments make it impossible for two successful females connected to the old narrative to coexist.

Self-confidence didn't come easily on the playground. In fact, it's not easy for adults either. But it's really an exercise in futility under the old narrative of patriarchy. It's pointless to think anything positive can result from something so negative when we rely on an old story told by men about women, as we seek to replace it with a new story. The relationship will always end with conflict or contention. In biblical terms, it's impossible to "put new wine into old wineskins because the old wineskins are not equipped to hold the fermentation expansion of the new wine."[1] Therefore, the old wineskins—our minds and mind-sets—must be emptied of all the old ways of thinking.

Every time a woman's self-esteem is based only on who or what she is attached to, patriarchy calls the shots. The only time the negative attributes of patriarchy aren't calling the shots in our actions is when our self-esteem is based on,

---

[1] Christina Fox, "When We Try to Put New Wine into Old Wineskins," January 14, 2015, https://www.iBelieve.com/Print/1172503g.

connected to, and valued by our connection to the master Creator of all things beautiful, right, and good: God alone.

Every time we fight with one another for position, status, or material gain; every time we treat one another as inferior in class or status, we play right into patriarchy's controlling grip. And every time we attack one another's outward appearances, real accomplishments, or earned opportunities, because we feel threatened or insecure, we reinforce the system that was created to divide and conquer us. Fortunately, the time when our survival and worth were directly linked to men is past.

Thousands of years ago, it was acceptable to compete for a man's approval when you were considered his property. You fought for a position for yourself and your children in a family system of multiple wives and (or) concubines sharing one man. This arrangement was necessary in order for the family to continue should the head of the household meet his end. Then as now, women wanted to secure a hopeful future for themselves and their children. But today we don't organize the family as a harem, and women's survival doesn't depend on who's next in line for the throne. So the unhealthy competition that was forced on us years ago has no place in today's society, or on its multiple playgrounds.

We now have an opportunity to seize the leadership in changing the narrative created by patriarchy and accepted by society all those years ago. We can do this by consistently and consciously fashioning a new theme for women, made up of our individual smaller stories of togetherness.

As little girls on the playground, we had no way to escape the power of patriarchy to dictate how we treated one another. And no one told us that the situations we saw on the playground would also play out in our adult lives.

Chapter 2

In the Presence of Our Past

Connecting the Dots

When the old ways are unhealthy and obsolete, the only way we can avoid living in the presence of our past is to acknowledge how business as usual has failed us. We need to replace old behaviors with new ways and practice them regularly and often. For a better look at what I'm saying, let's use the example of genetics and DNA, whose effects are transgenerational (that is, they cross generations).

Doctors use genetics to explain diseases and their potential to occur in families. It gives a picture of how our bodies are likely to respond to environmental conditions.

We can see the generational effects of genetics when we look at old family photos. We may have a striking resemblance to an aunt, uncle, cousin, or great-grandparent.

Because of genetics, eye color might skip a generation and show up again later. It's all in our DNA.

Some traits are guaranteed to show up again and again, across generations. However, others are passed down but don't appear. In other words, they can be avoided. They can be controlled by taking specific steps.

When I look in the mirror, my reflection reminds me of a photo of my mother taken more than sixty years ago. She was much younger at the time than I am now, but our eyes and facial expressions are the same. When I look at her photo, it's like I'm in the presence of my mother's past but seeing myself at the same time. Not only are my looks like hers, but some of her mannerisms, habits, and beliefs are alive in me. I can see patterns of behavior in me that I saw in my mother.

My mother has an entrepreneurial spirit. She's a spiritual entrepreneur, or spritualpreneur—my name for someone who creates her own platform for sharing her spirituality with others. But she also has a business mind-set for individual development and leadership that allowed her to pursue economic independence through education, innovation, creativity and planning. These traits were passed on to me directly when she shared her vision for independence and property ownership as well as her business plan. It's how she shaped my mind-set. Her professional, spiritual, and educational patterns of behavior became my patterns because I witnessed them.

When I reflect on how past generations influence our thoughts and actions, it's apparent that children respond to what we do rather than what we say. Our minds are conditioned to regard life as a result of what we saw and experienced in the past, so in that sense, the past is always present. Good or bad, we are constantly in the presence of our past and are heavily influenced by it. If our past was unhealthy, it will affect our present.

Footprints in the Sands of Time

Comparison, rivalry, bullying, competition and jealousy are the transgenerational DNA (Dysfunctional/Damaging Negative Actions) of foehood. When I think about foehood and its transgenerational DNA coding, it's like I am in the presence of patriarchy's past, but seeing myself or ourselves at the same time, reliving its generational effects, that we were groomed to participate in, over and over again.

Habits form in the past, whether distant past or recent past. American businessman, educator, and author Stephen Covey suggested that it only takes seven days to form a habit.[2] It takes just as much time and consistency to break that habit, and it takes repeated effort to replace an old habit with a new one. Covey reported that consistency is the key to successful change.

---

[2] Stephen Covey, *7 Habits of Highly Successful People* (New York: Free Press, 1989).

But what do we do if the habits we want to change were formed over a thousand years ago? Because the ways of patriarchy played out across multiple generations, does that mean we're doomed to live forever in the presence of our past? No, it doesn't. We're not doomed to live forever in the presence of our past if we're willing to make real changes. We're only doomed if we fail to *be* the change we want to see in today's society.

Change is always possible when the right activities and behaviors are consistently applied, even when the environment is less than healthy. So I'd like to believe we can create a new present.

As children, some of our behaviors were learned in our experiences with friends, family, and the community. But others were innate, already written on the tablets of our minds. These are the behaviors that made our parents say, "I don't know where she gets that." Whether innate or learned, certain behaviors and traits follow us from generation to generation.

Behavior that's been a habit for any length of time is very difficult to change because its influence becomes natural. Childhood situations in which we bullied others or were bullied ourselves can put us at risk of repeating that behavior in our adult lives if we haven't broken the habit. Of course, when we relive our past over and over again, it means the behaviors of the past are a symptom of a larger problem. For example, bullying often has its roots in a controlling mind-set. We have to look at their beginnings to understand how these mind-sets work and to identify solutions.

The most common problems in society today probably have their roots in some form of traumatic conflict. Responses to conflict in our society are often expressed as violence, one form of which is bullying. It's definitely not a new phenomenon that we've just stumbled upon. Bullying is aimed at those seen as inferior or weak, so children on the playground were perfect targets. Likewise, adults who are trying to establish their place in society are prime targets. The bully is looking for wholeness and self-preservation, all the while unaware of their own insecurity.

The Tragedies of the Past's Presence

A recent news article told of a nine-year-old girl who committed suicide. Police and family members believe she was bullied because of her friendship with a white boy. She was encouraged by the classmates who taunted her to "just die. You think you are white because you ride to school with that white boy."[3] This incident is tragic and is not isolated. It resembles hundreds of other incidents of bullying, and their effect on society is heartbreaking. For one thing, little boy or girl bullies always become big bullies, men or women, if

---

[3] Meghan Keneally, "Police Investigating Alleged Bullying in 9 Year Old Girl's Apparent Suicide," December 11, 2018, accessed 12/11/2018, https://abc-news.go.com.

they are not conscious or aware enough to break its behavior habits in their lives.

Most of us can probably recall a time when we or someone we know experienced this type of behavior. It happens in churches, workplaces, and community organizations. And it's time we recognize that these attitudes and behaviors spring from a powerful source—patriarchy. We can't remain silent and allow little girls to suffer like this one did.

Long before this little girl's body died, her spirit was already the victim of others who refused to accept her as she was *and* who didn't understand who they themselves were. By recognizing the systemic problem at work in this situation, we can get to the root of the problem and transform society. Rebuilding people's self-esteem will help to recondition our minds. The role of sisterhood is to fashion little girls who grow up to be adult women full of confidence. And to rebuild women, changing them from enemies into sisters.

A Foe's Point of View

Usually a bully sees his or her target as lacking in confidence, self-esteem, and self-worth. They consider this person to be inferior and weak. When I did my doctoral research on the impact of patriarchy on female leadership in the church, I discovered that patriarchy was at the root of many hostile interactions between women. I also learned that in most relationships observed between women, emotional and spiritual connection and pure women's intuition weren't celebrated, encouraged, or even mentioned. Sisterhood was strained, and patriarchal views appeared to permeate many women's minds, resulting in disconnection.

One way this showed up was women who ignored the obvious struggles of other women as a way to survive in the environments in which they operated. Many of the harmful psychological patterns seen in bullies are rooted in the values and system of patriarchy.

Another thing my research revealed about bullies was that many of them repeat abusive behaviors they witnessed or experienced earlier in life. The psychological impact on the bully's mind and attitude has damning consequences for his or her self-esteem and confidence, especially if the bully grew up in an unhealthy environment where positive coping skills weren't taught or modeled. If the bully witnessed some sort of abuse against a loved one, he or she might act out in violent ways against weaker persons.

Two forms of bullying common in the church are spiritual bullying and emotional bullying. The bully (1) undermines you and your ability to serve in a specific ministerial capacity; (2) resists cooperating with you unless it's on their own terms, especially if they have their eye on your position; (3) conveys to the leader their own expertise and your incompetence; and (4) is masterful at getting others to believe or buy into their rhetoric or disregard for the person or people they are trying to remove, replace, or spiritually and emotionally discredit or annihilate.

In the workplace, bullying often concerns qualifications and credibility. The bully (1) creates a toxic work environment, (2) tries to interfere with your being selected for assignments or promotion, and (3) creates communication barriers between you and your coworkers.

These are just two examples among the many that exist today. I'm sure you can think of others. The truth is that wherever it happens or whatever the circumstances, the bully is almost certainly in the presence of his or her past. It may be that their victim triggered the memory of some past event or pain that made the bully feel threatened in some way. To the foe, bullying you is their way of correcting a past wrong. They may be responding to something long ago or in the recent past (for example, last night before bed, in the morning before school, or last week).

The Lockup

The mental, emotional, spiritual, and overall inner impact of a stronger-versus-weaker mind-set and how that plays out in society was established long ago. The bully's need for control takes precedence over everything and everyone else as they seek to compensate for their own loss of control when they experienced bullying. So history repeats itself and reveals what being in the presence of our past looks like.

What if the bully's a girl or a woman who experienced violence at the hands of another girl or woman? That suggests that the environment she grew up in has left her with a need to feel confident in her surroundings and in herself. If this is the case, she may take any action necessary to ensure the particular kind of confidence she requires.

Being strong or capable or smart enough to control your situation or surroundings creates confidence. But when you're uncertain of your ability to protect yourself or your loved ones, you're thrust into survival mode as scripted by the norms established under patriarchy.

Strangely enough, the bully's intent to display confidence and strength really points to hidden insecurity. It has everything to do with their own lack of control, which they seek to regain by other means. And that other means can be attacking you and everything you stand for. Sometimes it involves violence because that might be the bully's go-to strategy. Keep in mind that violence isn't always physical. It can also be psychological as well as emotional, which is often worse because the impact lasts longer.

An adult bully's behavior is the same as a child's. That's why child bullies become adult bullies. They can't empathize with the person they see as inferior or weak because they've never corrected the psychological problems created by their own traumatic experiences of the past.

Same Image, Different Mirror

Whether you feel a threat to your emotional, spiritual, or psychological survival, the state you're in is more like a bridge that brings us together as sisters than a gulf that separates us and pits us against one another as foes. The ability to empathize or relate to others is key to freeing a bully from his or her insecurity.

The mind-sets we've developed throughout our lives are made up of many pieces. We have a natural drive to survive, and we react to threats instinctively by repeating behaviors we've seen or experienced in the past. When it comes to survival, it doesn't matter whether our instincts are good or bad. So we don't think about their consequences for others.

History has ways of repeating itself. In some faith traditions, these are known as generational curses or generational blessings. Both curses and blessings suggest that in any given moment for any given situation, we're always living in the presence of our past, influenced by a curse or a blessing.

A generational curse grows out of bad habits, behaviors, rituals, and even health practices or problems that follow a family bloodline from generation to generation. The concept applies to ideas and beliefs that appear in business and religious establishments. One example of an unhealthy habit is smoking. Some families have entire generations of smokers.

It's one of the reasons insurance companies and doctors ask us about our family histories.

As I look at how our past constantly influences our present in various ways, I'm reminded of certain biblical narratives and concepts in the Christian tradition. The concept of a generational curse represents a way of understanding why people act the way they act. It can answer questions like what, when, where, why, and how a person's behavior, habits, and health problems originated. According to author Marilyn Hickey, a generational curse is "an uncleaned iniquity that increases in strength from generation to generation to the next, affecting the members of that family and all who come into relationship with that family."[4]

The Past's Power to Rob Futures

The Bible contains many examples of weaknesses and hereditary traits passed down through a family's bloodline. For example, in the Old Testament story of the brothers Cain and Abel, Cain murdered his brother out of jealousy. Cain committed murder because he didn't get what he wanted. Afterward, he didn't have a change of heart or mind, nor did he ask for forgiveness.

According to Christian belief, we express sincere regret and remorse by admitting the wrongdoing (sin) and by a

---

[4] Marilyn Hickey, *Breaking Generational Curses: Overcoming the Legacy of Sin in Your Family* (Tulsa, OK: Harrison House Publishing, 2000).

changed heart. When we do, God's punishment can be avoided or softened. However, failure to repent not just for our own misdeeds but also those of our forebears (generational repentance) can have consequences that recur over and over again. Our descendants may repeat the same behaviors, and those practices, traits, and mind-sets will follow them. Today, women (and girls) and men (and boys) still commit murder due to jealousy; and women (and girls) and men (and boys) are murdered due to jealousy.

Another biblical example of a family's generational curse is Jacob's theft of his brother Esau's inheritance through deceit. Jacob tricked his brother into giving away his inheritance by taking advantage of Esau's weakness and his need to survive in that moment.

It is possible for good to emerge from the ashes of wrong. Jacob repented and was renamed Israel. This change of action and identification brought about embraced favor and blessings that still exist and is seen today. Therefore, not every generational curse will bring harm when family members make better choices than earlier generations did. But it helps to be aware of the risk associated with certain habits: emotional; psychological; physiological; spiritual and hereditary traits.

We can use the same kind of analysis used by medical and insurance professionals to identify people with tendencies toward certain behaviors. Not to alienate or reject them but to understand who they are from a spiritual and emotional perspective. Before a situation can be corrected, we must be aware of the situation, the person, and the history so the right steps are taken. We want to avoid that which created the problem in the first place.

Breaking the Sisterhood Curse

A generational curse can only be broken when we acknowledge failure within ourselves and our families and correct the behavior. Replacing the DNA and harmful habits or traits we may have inherited with positive ones will promote self-confidence and self-esteem. In today's society, we see the result of generations of families living under the curses of their past. Jews are still hated by the descendants of Esau. Blacks are hated too. And women are still abused, scorned, and to some degree controlled by patriarchy.

All this discord has a powerful impact on society's psyche, and we need to eliminate it once and for all. We can get to a place of mutual respect even though we disagree, and a sisterhood based not on friendship (because friendship involves choice) but simply on the fact that we are women.

The Monster of It All

The elephant in society's room is a monster! And it gets stronger with each generation, wreaking havoc with women's relationships and preventing authentic sisterhood. Because this state of affairs has been steadfastly ignored or denied, the monster grows bigger all the time. And the lies we were told about one another and the status quo they create becomes a vehicle for *foehood* in society and in our lives as women.

Every assault against women, especially by other women, increases the power of these lies. These lies are so broad that it's hard to get around, and their power so deeply rooted that we can't get under it. The walls are high and massive. Until now, we knew nothing of what we were up against and the divisions created between us. We didn't know that when we treated one another as enemies, we were acting out of values and belief systems intended to prevent our unity.

One reason an illness like cancer spreads is the disbelief that it's real. The signs are ignored, and what started out small and isolated becomes unmanageable—perhaps too late. Another reason is fear. We close our eyes and act like nothing's wrong, while the damage continues unchecked. We say to ourselves, *Maybe it will go away.* But when we finally give in and seek help, we risk being told it's too late.

I see the effects of patriarchy on society—especially women—as a cancer that's been ignored for thousands of years. As a result, it's become a ravenous beast that's spread throughout our families, our institutions, our workplaces, and our churches. Instead of bonding through shared experiences, support for one another, and harmony in sisterhood (even when we disagree), we're scarred by the past, by the narratives that shaped us but didn't allow our input.

Women have different opinions, ideas, goals, dreams, sorrows, and life experiences. To understand one another as individuals, we must first understand the stories behind the experiences that shaped us, or perhaps how our families influenced us. We can understand one another individually only by understanding the families or groups we came from. When we fail to realize what we have in common, our relationships are strained, and sisterhood is threatened or dies. It seems to me this is already happening. But restoration is possible if we ask the right questions of society and ourselves and face the answers without fear or shame.

Perhaps the first question we should ask is, Why do we seem to be stuck in the presence of our past—the cruelty of patriarchy? For one thing, no one reported this disease in society that should have been dealt with before it became an outright plague. It goes on infecting women with its abuse and encourages society to mistreat women and women to mistreat one another.

Earlier, I talked about generational curses that show up in families. Grandmothers, grandfathers, mothers, fathers, daughters, sons, and other family members are all affected in some way, even when some generations are skipped. These traits can be passed down through a family's descendants, which is why their impact is so strong and so striking.

The Bible tells us that without sincere expression of regret, sorrow, and repentance, the sins of the father will afflict a family's third and fourth generations. I'd like to suggest that patriarchy's descendants aren't just weaknesses and trickery and the other DNA recognized in foehood but also the exercise of control, which took root as an evil presence hanging over all of society.

As we struggle to rise above our past and overcome the bad habits we've inherited, we have to realize that we're trying to win the fight against patriarchy and its by-products with an obsolete mind-set. Patriarchy struts around in our schools, our institutions, our workplaces, and our churches, poisoning our behavior and our interactions with one another.

Chapter 3

Unhealthily Ever After

In the Fight of Our Lives

What we do know is that women have been battling this system for a long time. We've fought for equality in positions, pay, and certain matters of preference or choice. We've accomplished great things even though it's been an uphill battle all the way, but we still struggle for equality in many areas. Individuals have given voice to these grave concerns, but until now, no voice has arisen to address the areas of struggle that remain. They seem to have gone unnoticed or unmentioned or both. As a result, our sisterhood has been left in a deplorable state.

I'm not sure whether what I'm about to say is too shameful for us to acknowledge collectively or whether it just hurts too much to talk about it. Either way, it's time we brought it up because it's left our sisterhood crippled despite all we've achieved and continue to achieve at work and in church and civic organizations. We've been brainwashed into thinking that relating to one another on an emotional level (especially in matters of competition and survival) makes us less competent than men. It's left us confused about whether we should use our innate gifts of emotion and intuition with one another or ignore these connections just to appease the existing stereotypes about us.

You see, we were led to believe that emotional *detachment* is a good strategy for interacting with one another. At least it kept us from being invisible when the few of us who "made it" were allowed to sit at the boardroom table with men (and other women) and to be considered for advancement (and therefore survival) in our chosen fields.

We came to feel that if we were going to survive in a man's world, we had to do what men did, even if it meant doing it to one another. Relating to one another with detachment proved that we were tough enough to be measured against men. For those of us trying to advance in corporate America, a tough exterior was seen as a sure way to achieving upper-level management status. Sure it was a chance at leadership, but the part was already scripted by a system designed for men's convenience only. And corporate America is a world where the ratio of men and women in leadership is always to our disadvantage.

We *have* made great strides as females in leadership. But given the environment in which we've had to fight to survive, we must redefine how we see one another by renouncing the autocratic system of patriarchy.

More and more, we've been entrepreneurs who created our own business platforms and opportunities for ourselves and others. We've contributed greatly to our economy and our community, impacting our families' quality of life directly and positively. And though we've done all this while navigating the minefields of patriarchy, we have bigger fish to fry. We're the only ones who can do it, and it must be done collectively if we're to make our relationships better and our sisterhood stronger.

As we established ourselves in our workplaces, civic organizations, and church settings, in some ways we disestablished ourselves as allies by allowing the lies of patriarchy to restrict our interactions and experiences with one another. Yes, we've proven that we can be successful and even lead successfully, but our behavior has demonstrated that we buy into the lies we were told.

In my opinion, this is a problem because we're conditioned to use *his* terms to define us and *his* beliefs to relate to one another. In the process, we've adopted certain behaviors and attitudes about ourselves and one another, whether those relationships are professional, personal, or spiritual.

Some behaviors that are common among women are seen as weak or lacking leadership quality when it comes to getting ahead. We've been forced to tread lightly in some environments where strength means lack of feeling or emotional connection. Connection to anyone or anything less than strong was considered a sign of weakness or insecurity. We were encouraged to ignore our feelings and the feelings of others in order to reach certain goals.

This hard-hearted existence forced on us by patriarchy was not meant to nurture positive female relationships. It was intended to do just the opposite. It was (and is) authoritative at its core and causes discord between sisters, women, and girls: *us*. The wishes, opinions, needs, and wants of women certainly weren't taken into account. So if you ever wonder how some people, groups, organizations, and even leaders came to be so unfeeling and so domineering, you only need to look at the system that bred this behavior in the first place.

I'm not saying that strong leadership styles are wrong or bad altogether. But I am saying let's be aware of their origin and how lack of feeling can be more destructive than beneficial for people, groups, and societies. What society needs more of is kindness, especially when we're supposed to be people of faith who claim to be grounded in *love*.

From a historical viewpoint, under patriarchy we often didn't know or even *want* to know the women with whom we had relationships. The relationships were forced, and I believe this fostered a spirit of resistance that's still with us today. For example, we might resist giving a new woman a chance in social or professional situations. Not because we don't like her but because pressure to accept her can cause real discomfort.

I call this a transgenerational spirit of resistance. It was ushered in by patriarchy, but its powerful impact is still with us today. It hinders us in ways we never thought about. So it's up to us to fight back against this conditioned response with a new type of sisterhood, the opposite of what our minds have been conditioned to accept as our norm. Because patriarchy was not created to support positive relationships between women, it conditioned us to believe the following:

- Women and girls are supposed to compete with one another for attention or affirmation, especially from men.
- Women and girls aren't supposed to get along with one another.
- Women and girls are to be compared to one another in terms of looks, income, status, position, and so on.
- It's okay for women and girls to ignore other women's and girls' feelings.

All lies! But we've been blindly operating on autopilot ever since this autocratic system began. We've been ignoring our collective emotional connections, and that's the only way the influence of patriarchy has survived among us for so long.

Created Opponents

If you're looking for historical examples of how we were positioned in society to compete with one another, consider the biblical story of Rachel and Leah. The two were bio-logical sisters, identified right from the start by their looks. They knew who met the beauty standards of their time and who didn't, and they knew that high value was placed on their bodies. They were encouraged to do whatever was necessary to please men—their father and their intended husband.

These ladies were biological sisters, yet they were kept from being true sisters in any way that failed to appease "the system"—their father and their husband. Rachel and Leah were sisters, but they became opponents too because they were married to the same man. They were trapped by the need to satisfy men, prisoners of a system that produced insecurity for women. And only relationships with men could relieve that insecurity.

Look at Hannah and Peninnah. These women were his-torical sister/wives married to the same man. Valued by their connection to him. They were also valued by their ability to have children. However, one (Hannah) couldn't have chil-dren at first. The other (Peninnah) could have children and did. Peninnah taunted Hannah constantly regarding her in-ability to conceive children. She even suggested that Hannah had somehow fell out of favor with God. Both women were aware of the value placed on them by society (patriarchy).

Take another look at the biblical story of Sarah and Hagar. Another historical narrative that illustrates how women were encouraged and even expected to compete with and antagonize one another is unveiled right here. As the story suggests, there was no room for compassion and understanding between the two women. Our God-given ability to understand and show compassion is the very essence of our being. But Sarah was eager to please her husband and submit to the system in operation at that time, so she took matters into her own hands.

We now live in the presence of Sarah and Hagar's past, the presence of Rachel and Leah's past and the presence of Hannah and Peninnah's past. With the exception of Hannah's gracious treatment of Peninnah given their unhealthy environment, the reason these women couldn't and didn't choose to act differently is because they were only as valuable as the men they were attached to. They were only as free as men's authority granted them to be free.

God's Displeasure toward Foehood

In Old Testament times, evicting a woman from the family and leaving her alone with a baby was a death sentence for both of them. Hagar had no family and no resources, and she was the sole breadwinner for herself and her child. But God not only showed up and revealed Himself as their provider but also demonstrated His opposition to the mistreatment of women.

God met Hagar where she was, trying to survive. Trying to deal with the humiliation she'd been dealt. Trying to handle being alone in the world. And trying to understand how God could abandon her. As a woman, I can relate to Hagar. We can all relate.

Hagar's Story / God's Mercy

Sarah and Abraham weren't the only ones God provided for in this story. God told Hagar that He was going to bless her with many descendants through her son Ishmael. Sarah's success came at the expense of Hagar's hurt and pain, yet Hagar's success was also rooted in suffering. And we have no record of her voice or Sarah's.

Hannah's Story / God's Mercy

Peninnah was not the only one God responded to. Hannah suffered at the hands of another oppressed woman. Disconnected to the impact of her actions against Hannah, Peninnah was taught to believe through the system of patriarchy that only through the hurt of another woman could her value, worth and self-esteem increase and count and identify her as one with favor with God and man. However, God, understanding a system that divided these two women, did not allow the taunting to continue. He gave Hannah a son too. And not just any son but a child who would do mighty and great things. The Love of God in this story championed the value of both women. Yes at different times and due to different levels of learning but still in His time He responded to Hannah's trust in Him and her well-mannered character which did not appear to allow her to treat her rival in similar ways of discord.

What We Didn't Know

Success in an autocratic system like patriarchy is certainly possible for women. All throughout history, right up to today, we've seen successful women. But if your success depends on your sisters' humiliation and pain, those relationships will always be strained. Communication will be stressful, and real sisterhood can never be achieved.

These six women and their stories illustrate how we've been living unhealthily ever after. But they also show that even in the most toxic environments, God keeps His promise to protect, bless, and provide for women. Most of all, He'll break through any system to prove that He doesn't love any one of us more than the others. It's His desire that we're treated with love, grace, and mercy—not deception.

As women living in a society where our minds are controlled and our emotions are restricted, it's hard to believe that God wants to break through this autocratic system of patriarchy and change things on our behalf. But I believe He wants us to change our relationships with one another by discarding the old narratives of patriarchy. It means changing what we believe about us and what we think and say about one another. It's called sisterhood. And yes God supports it.

Why does it start with us—women, sisters, girls, even those who identify as girls at heart? It starts here with us because our voices were silenced and ignored. And when we did finally speak, we used words that were given to us instead of our own. Relationships that could have been completely authentic were distorted by the lies we were told. When we spoke or acted, it was like we could only regurgitate what we were taught.

We've learned to ignore one another's feelings in order to survive. In controlled environments, we learned to be loyal to the system and not one another. We feared being doomed to failure, abandonment, and hopelessness if we didn't toe the line. We also feared losing support from our families and our friends.

Why didn't our voices matter? Why didn't we support one another? I can only guess. Perhaps we believed we were serving a greater good. But that greater good's turned out to be preservation of society's dominant voices, opinions, and desires, and men's security. Besides our separation from one another, our silence and our submission made men feel more confident and secure. But just as men's security shouldn't be threatened by our unity, our security shouldn't depend on other women's humiliation and shame.

What they told us over and over again is that to survive, we have to turn away from one another and toward the system that created the false narrative. But the problem with suppressing one person's voice is that collective success isn't possible without the benefit of other voices. We are relational people, created to be in relationship with God and with others. And the system of patriarchy is responsible for disrupting this arrangement. The breakdown of society has left us living unhealthily ever after.

Society offers many examples that prove my point. First let's look at some of the results we deal with daily in all our social organizations, including the church.

Ever since patriarchy took over society, our interactions with one another have been troubled. Families, businesses, and churches have been affected by how we were conditioned to think. Patterns of behavior that involve rivalry produced unnatural competition. The consequences of rivalry—rage, murder, bullying, and silencing—have left terrible scars on our lives.

Unfortunately, no matter how ugly these acts are, they keep happening and even increasing. To make matters worse, the effects have spilled over into the religious community as well. It's embedded into how society thinks, and members of society attend our churches.

The spread of patriarchy's attitudes and beliefs illustrates how completely it's entrenched in our society. For example, sex trafficking of women for profit and pleasure is a direct outcome of patriarchy. Some people think it's okay when women's voices are silenced because it must mean they consent to their circumstances. Or their silence lessens the guilt of the guilty. Therefore, women in this situation are drugged by their captors as a means of control.

Forced Adaptation

We've been forced to accept patriarchy's standards for how we're treated by men and by one another. We've adopted certain assumptions about how society expects us to treat one another and relate to one another. So far, unhealthily ever after has been the result.

Destructive conflict is another social wound inflicted by patriarchy. Conflict is natural but not when it's expressed as physical abuse, control, and even murder. These forms of violence are part of the unhealthily ever after of our times. For years, people denied the ability of patriarchy to control our thinking in ways that harm us and how it destroys true sisterhood by depicting a false norm.

We see many examples of this unhealthily-ever-after syndrome in society. The one that's most crucial to our present and future as leaders of a new sisterhood movement is the lie that says we can't operate outside the system of patriarchy. But it's not that sisterhood is doomed, it's just that we didn't know how badly it was damaged and how it happened in the first place. Instead of bringing us together to oppose it, this narrative has in fact kept us apart and is more powerful than any of us realized.

So what has living unhealthily ever after done to sisterhood, and what do we need to do about it? I'm suggesting that this land we've been conditioned to live in has distorted our relationships both in the past and in the present. Unless we change where our thoughts and feelings reside, our future relationships and interactions will be false as well.

We were positioned as opponents because of our close proximity and common needs. We were pitted against one another yet simultaneously linked together under patriarchy's script, and that distorted our true selves and our precious voices. It was meant to guarantee power, pleasure, submission, and unchallenged control over half of society's population. The female population.

Submission to its will without challenging or questioning what we've been conditioned to believe and become in this land of unhealthily ever after means that pleasure exists only for those in control. The result is what I call *foehood*—a false and perverted version of sisterhood (or, depending on the facts, circumstance or context, brotherhood or male/female relationships) in an unhealthy environment.

Chapter 4

The Foehood Experience

L ife can be, and really is, extremely demanding. If you pair life's demands with family responsibilities what you will see is a woman's patience, skills, and obligations being stretched across multiple situations. Sometimes being stretched to the limit.

I am saying it like this to bring reality to the fact that not all perceived foehood experiences are actual foehood experiences. Sometimes a woman (or girl) can, for example, look in your direction but not see you because she is thinking about or responding mentally to so many different crisis or situations. Thus, her actions, or reactions, as well as responses towards you are not deliberate or personal.

These matters should and must be (individually) evaluated very carefully and with acceptance and understanding of the other person's situation. However, when this is not the case foehood happens and sometimes it is both deliberate and personal.

I am ashamed to say that foehood happens often—daily—and has a very subtle way of forcing its way into our thoughts, minds, and actions toward one another. It is extremely sneaky and is fueled and empowered by the disguise that it puts on proudly. It's brutal. It doesn't feel good at all. Sometimes it even makes you feel like you won't survive the power of its cruelty. There are moments when you feel abandoned and isolated. And then there are times when it makes you angry and even sad. It's not comfortable. It wears a disguise called opinion. But this opinion is very strong; it lacks compassion and has no understanding of how it can be used as a deadly weapon.

I'm talking about when someone feels the need to express their *very strong opinion* against you to the point where it's not really an opinion at all. It's judgment—judgment against what you wear, how you look, what you've done, why you did it, what you should've done … and the list goes on and on.

Strong opinions are good. We all have them, and we always will. But when your opinion disguises your judgment of another woman who may not be your friend or your choice or whatever, it threatens the bonds of sisterhood and encourages foehood. I call this the beginning stages of a foehood experience.

The Judgment Seat

Nothing can prevent us from being judged by others. All we have to do is walk into a place where other people are present, and right away we'll be evaluated, labeled, and grouped because of how we look, what we're wearing, and how others perceive us. Judgment is based on each person's beliefs, values, and frames of reference, and it can be quite harsh depending on who's doing the judging.

When you're used to being judged, it has a way of throwing you into an automatic defensive mode. This can lead us to believe we must always be vigilant, on alert. The constant feeling that we have to justify our actions and motives makes us go to great lengths to make sure no one misrepresents us. And whenever we are misrepresented in any way, it understandably awakens the anger, resentment, and intolerance already planted in our minds by patriarchy.

Most of us aren't aware of how patriarchy is responsible for our negative thoughts, feelings, and behavior. Long ago, our minds were colonized by the ways we were conditioned to think, and that corrupted our emotional being. It's made us more apt to be offended by even the most innocent and well-intentioned words and actions. Long ago, patriarchy took away the following:

- our authentic voice
- our sense of control
- our genuine sisterhood

Today we still see how these losses impact us and contribute powerfully to the judgments of foehood. I think of each of these three missing elements as a quarter of our being. Three-quarters of our being is missing, and one-quarter is left struggling to understand why it's so easy to be intolerant, angry, resentful, and sometimes even hostile toward one another. We're in the fight of our lives more often than we may care to admit.

The Struggle to Understand

I often wonder why we take offense at one another so quickly and seemingly at the most innocent things. For example, in the workplace, a female supervisor might instruct you to take a specific action in order to meet a project deadline. But you perceive it as a personal attack on your know-how and skills, and you resist cooperating.

A case like this points straight back to our authentic voice that was stolen from us long ago, not to mention our sense of control and our genuine sisterhood. But for the hijacking of these three important elements, we probably wouldn't react defensively in the above situation but would accept the suggestion without pushing back.

Our authentic voice, sense of control, and true sisterhood are essential to our emotional well-being. When we don't have them, it triggers a tendency toward foehoodism and pushes us even farther from sisterhood. If you think about it, it makes sense.

Anyone who feels silenced will resist—against their boss, their pastor, their teacher, their friend—even when that person happens to be a woman. Anyone who feels out of control will push back with resentment and hostility. And any woman who's insensitive toward other women will be inclined to lash out in opposition when she feels threatened. It's a natural reaction.

But in fact the real threats to our emotional, physical, and spiritual survival are actually the values and beliefs of patriarchy, not one another. They've defined us and conditioned us to behave in certain ways. It's time to end our resignation to these views we were forced to adopt—views about one another—and create a new system that opposes this system at every turn.

The Mechanics of Foehood

Our assimilation into the belief system of patriarchy and the way we were forced to conform to it has taken a heavy toll on sisterhood. Often we give each other a kind of rough justice. The stress we feel now is what women have felt throughout history, and when their voices were silenced, they lashed out against those closest to them—one another. Because they didn't know any better, they went for the nearest target. It left them (and now us) upset with one another and not knowing why.

It started early, when we were young and innocent, when we were little girls trying to grow up. As the patterns traveled with us into middle school, high school, and college, we saw the effects more and more as we found our way into various social groups. Ironically, these groups, through their values and characteristics, enacted the same system of forced adaptation as patriarchy. Members are expected to conform, and outsiders' opinions, needs, desires, and wants are dismissed. As in patriarchy, only the leader decides.

Once it gets started, the energy of foehood is circular and goes around and around like a merry-go-round. When I said earlier that it's the same image in a different mirror, I meant that patriarchy shows up over and over as we keep having the same experiences. We never get off the hamster wheel. And once again, there's that same straight line between the workings of patriarchy and rivalry among women.

The Pettiness of Foehood

As mentioned at the beginning of this chapter, all matters of interaction must and should be examined carefully and with acceptance and understanding in order to determine the type of experience you may be having. Realistically asking the question: is this a foehood experience or not, in light of the multiple situations and demands placed on women (and girls) on a daily basis:

Unfortunately, in the course of our ordinary day-to-day activities, we've all run into people who are excessively concerned with the latest gossip. They can't resist weighing in on how you look, who you're with, what you did, and what you wore when you did it. Even how you sound is of real interest to some for no apparent reason except to express their unhelpful and unsolicited strong opinion, disregard, or perhaps judgment. Here are a few examples.

Experience 1: It's your first day on the job, and you walk into the office with a positive attitude and a brand-new outfit in honor of the occasion. You even have a cheerful outlook toward the new people you're meeting for the first time … and it happens. For no clear reason at all, some woman gives you the cold shoulder. Doesn't respond to your greeting. You struggle to understand because all you did was enter the scene in a pleasant mood.

Experience 2: What about this? You've had your current job for years, and you're doing very well. Because of your skill at handling projects with professionalism and meeting deadlines, you're the subject of office gossip about how you think you're smarter or better than your coworkers. Or more disturbing, if you have a good rapport with a male boss, you might be suspected of having slept your way to the top. If your boss is a woman, perhaps you earned brownie points by doing unmentionable things that aren't discussed in polite company.

Experience 3: Picture a time when you went to a social or political function. The scene is full of other professionals, church members or organization members as interested as you are in the events' purpose. The only difference is it's your first time. You don't know anyone, but they all seem to know one another. They have professional, social and religious affiliation or contact with the leaders or sponsors of the event. But because you're the new unknown person, they don't seem to welcome you into their influential circle. They don't seem interested in knowing who you are or what you might bring to the table. You walk around feeling isolated and out of place, not understanding why, because it was a women's event, and it was attended by lots of enthusiastic women just like you.

Experience 4: What about walking into a new church? It's your first visit, and you're excited about the possibility of finding a new religious community. During the passing of the peace or whatever welcome ritual they practice, you move to greet someone by sharing a smile or a friendly blessing. But you're left feeling somehow uncomfortable and unwelcome.

You are confused because you received the cold shoulder from the women (or girl) you tried to embrace or greet.

Experience 5: What if you're dating someone, in a serious relationship, or even married? In any of these cases, what if other women in the community, in your church, or at your job know what your relationship status is? When the two of you appear together in public, do other women (or girls) pass you by deliberately and give their attention to the man (or boy) without the least acknowledgment of or apology to you?

Experience 6: What if you don't wear any symbol of commitment like a wedding or engagement ring and you're having an innocent conversation with a man who may be either married or single? If you're single, you're automatically labeled, instantly judged as flirting with, chasing after, or trying to get a man or seduce someone else's partner just because you're single.

Perhaps you may have had more drastic encounters that involved physical fighting, disloyalty where another woman who you called a friend, slept with or tried to sleep with your partner. There are so many common relatable examples. If you can relate to any of these examples or if they bring up memories of deliberate disrespect and disregard by another woman, you've been the victim of a foehood experience. A foehood experience is an incident characterized by non-cordial, not nice, lacking mutual respect, or hostile encounters instead of respectful exchanges. The term represents the brutal ways we may treat one another and think about one another, with behaviors that go back a long way. Not knowing that patriarchy was the root of the problem, we blamed one another instead. There will be many more examples and experiences created if we, as women in leadership of any kind, don't address the issues that our relationships with one another critically face. There will be many more experiences similar to these or even more drastic, especially among our young girls.

My Role in This Foehood Cycle

If we look back on our individual experiences, we'll find we have many in common. It should be grounds for compassion or at least respect. But perhaps it's not. Besides the times you were on the receiving end of a foehood experience, think about times when you may have contributed to someone else's. Sure, it's easy to say you've never done it. Most of us have a hard time admitting guilt.

But if you've ever at any time, even for a brief moment, looked down on another woman because of how she looked or what she wore or the neighborhood she came from or who her mother and father were, and after you looked down on her, you spoke unkindly about her or dismissed her or discarded or disregarded her or acted against her in any way because of your judgments concerning anything about her, you ... I ... we all had a hand in her foehood experience.

If you've ever disliked, critically judged, or secretly or publicly bashed a woman because her race, ethnicity, religion, facial features or physical or outward appearance was

- too sharp,
- too keen,
- too broad,
- too dark,
- too light,
- too fat, or
- too skinny

and treated her accordingly, you've participated in her foehood experience. If you've ever blamed a woman for being harassed or raped or abused without a thought to what she might have gone through or how she came to be in a dangerous situation in the first place, and if you judged her or spoke unkindly about her or treated her with disrespect, then you've participated in her foehood experience.

If you ever pretended to be another woman's confidante and then turned around and shared the secrets she held dear and entrusted to you, and it really hurt or damaged her in any way, then you've played a role in her foehood experience.

The reason I'm itemizing all these common experiences is to illustrate how easy it is to live in the land of foehood. It's very important to see how the system of patriarchy has found its way into even the most innocent interactions that are common in everyday life.

You may say, "Okay, I've had hostile thoughts about other women, but I've never acted on them." Well, my response is that we even have to guard our minds against the brainwashing we were subjected to long ago.

Many books have been written about the power of positive thinking. It's a concept founded on the biblical principle that says as you think in your heart and mind, so you are, so you will become, and most significantly, so you will act. We have to be careful what we think about one another because our thoughts can take on a life of their own. And before we know it, the whole world can see what's on our minds by the way we act.

This has been going on for centuries, and we've all witnessed it or experienced it but couldn't put our finger on what it was. I'm encouraging women everywhere to call it what it is and begin the movement to stamp it out in true leadership fashion.

Maybe not every woman on the planet deserves your "like," because after all, we do have our own personal and legitimate preferences. But all of us should be willing to give every woman respect. I'm not talking about the respect you give a friend, because how much effort does that take? I'm talking about respect that takes effort because it's the women we don't know who suffer the foehoodism. You should give respect just because she's a woman!

At our core, all of us have the same basic needs for food, clothing, and shelter. But we also need love, happiness, support, and respect. If you carefully look at the foehood scenarios described in this chapter and think about what I said in previous chapters, you'll notice a straight line. The line goes from you as a woman to the system that colonized your mind in the first place.

For example, judging a woman by her looks goes back to a time when women had to compete for attention or stand out from the rest in the eyes of men for the sake of survival. Beauty standards were defined under patriarchy, which places distinct value on outward appearances, especially where women are concerned.

The Birthing ... the Birthright

Judging a woman's worth based on how she does or doesn't dress, what she does or doesn't have, or what she has or hasn't done happens when we feel that our survival is being threatened. This is how we were conditioned to think—that our value increases when someone else's value decreases.

It's a mind-set that says *I have the right to act this way and think this way; I have the right to do whatever I want to do to her whenever I want to do it if she has something I want or something I don't have or if she's with someone I like or don't like.* That's the whole idea behind patriarchy.

This judgmental attitude was first used against women by men to ensure order in society. It emerged at a time when multiple families lived in the same household and gender role assignments were set in stone. But in time, it became a sinister habit that women themselves were brainwashed into adopting. It's become our go-to reaction whenever we perceive a threat to our status and feel a need to preserve our ego.

Unfortunately, the ego is based on outward things. Now that we're alert to what's been going on, we can begin to use the principles established and implemented by God. In my faith tradition, we are all very important to Him, both individually and collectively.

Thankfully, not all men buy into the patriarchy viewpoint. In spite of what we see in society today, you and I both know this because we've been cheered on by our husbands, fathers, brothers, friends, and colleagues. Many of them thoroughly support us, so don't think this book is about blaming men. It's not. This book is about a system that taught them to be the way they are. They too have been brainwashed by a system of gender assignments put in place to ensure social order and control.

From Brainwashed to Renewed

The only reason we have foehood experiences in the first place is because of the brainwashing that's gone on for generations. We were conditioned to see other women as threats to our survival. We fell for the lie that it's our norm. But when we participate in someone else's foehood experience, it's really because she reminds us of our own feelings of inadequacy, learned long ago and deeply embedded in our psyche. It comes from a past when we had to fight among ourselves to eat, sleep, and just plain exist.

The conflict wasn't created *by* us; it was created *for* us. However, if we keep holding on to patriarchy's beliefs and values in terms of how we treat one another, we're surrendering to its control over us instead of taking control over it and establishing a new form of engagement.

I think of this new form of engagement as a new level of female leadership that hasn't been tried until now. At first, this will be our challenge alone, because society can't change itself outwardly until we change inwardly.

The Control Factor

The foehood experience is also an act of control in which only the desires and needs of the dominant party are of interest. Sad to say, all this time while we've been living under this system and participating in someone else's foehood experience to gain and maintain control, the system itself steadily gained control over us. The only way to free ourselves is to rid ourselves, our society, and our hood of women of the foehood experience.

I came up with the term foehood to distinguish between our interactions under patriarchy and sisterhood (which I will redefine later). I want to be very specific about what I'm proposing here. So far, I've given you a broad view, but before I make a clear distinction between foehood and sisterhood, I need to reiterate a few realities.

What We Know

We've been living under an old definition of who we really are and what we can truly become. We're nothing like the lies they told about us. The dominant figures in society set us up to see one another as opponents, and because of that, our relationships with one another have been on a steady decline.

We were conditioned to see ourselves and one another in terms of external value—worthless unless attached to someone or something seen as greater in value. Our respect for one another as women has been critically damaged and is at an all-time low.

We now have an obligation to ourselves, one another, and society to model a higher level of respect. Not the kind of respect we give our families and friends but a respect that says, *Whether or not I know you personally, I will not allow any negative thinking to interfere with my regard for you. Some of your experiences were meant to destroy your mind, body, and feelings. But you're still standing, so I'll honor your strength because you're a survivor. You have a story, whether I know it or not, and you deserve my respect.*

You see, moving from foehood to sisterhood requires an even greater regard for another woman's experience. Not because you actually know her life story but because you know that all women and girls have a valid story. Despite the adversity she's faced, she has a voice. And that gives her innate value, whether or not we agree with how she handled her challenges.

When we understand this, we can make the transition from foehood to sisterhood.

Chapter 5

From Foehood to Sisterhood

Women (and girls) are in a state of emergency. Our collective action is required because our relationships with one another have been declining and strained for years, and unless something is done, they'll be beyond repair.

We might have women whom we consider our closest loyal friends. But it doesn't change the fact that women and girls battle relationship issues among themselves on a daily basis. That's because foehood shows up between women and girls who may or may not be acquainted, but definitely aren't friends. And there are historical reasons for this.

Going back to our days on the playground, strained relationships have been the rule and not the exception. That's because society influences us to operate as foes instead of sisters. Yet three of our most valuable and natural characteristics are our ability to do the following:

1. Connect on a spiritual level
2. Understand intuitively
3. Relate emotionally

These are innate skills, and we use them easily within our circle of friends. But at times we behave the opposite way in our personal dealings with one another and especially those outside our familiar circle of friends. We employ anger, intolerance, and resentment, or plan old dislike.

It doesn't take much effort to use our natural gifts, which are also our greatest strengths, among women we know and with whom we share a bond of mutual affection. They're usually part of our core personal groups in our church groups, our social clubs like sororities, and colleagues from work that we hang out with on a personal level. In other words, those we affectionately call "girlfriend." However, the hood of women is much bigger than our chosen circles, and respect for them demands more effort.

Our relationships can be salvaged only by enacting a new style of leadership. It involves commitment to women we might not know personally. But the fact that, like us, she's a woman or a girl living in a tough world full of difficult relationships turns our conflict into connection and transforms her from foe to sister. We are linked by our common interest in raising the level of respect we show one another, not because we're friends but because we're women.

Being friends is great! But it's not enough. We must remember our common bond of stories, experiences, disappointments, pain, and victories with other women who aren't necessarily our friends. Without a full and frank discussion, the gulf that exists between us will expand and pull us farther apart instead of bringing us together. Foehood will intensify, and true sisterhood will fade away.

Friendship versus Sisterhood

There are distinct differences between friendship and sisterhood. Both are valuable, but one happens by choice, and the other is a product of heritage or other ties.

As a matter of individual choice, being friends takes deliberate action and some degree of time commitment. Getting to know someone is a gradual process and requires an exchange of personal information. Both parties should be willing participants. Being or becoming friends also takes a degree of humility to form the initial bond. The resulting emotional connection between the parties is called friendship.

Because we have friends, it's hard for many of us to see or accept the need for true sisterhood. So it's been ignored and threatened and is now in a critical state. You can never befriend all the women in the world, but on some level, your story will be similar to all the women in the world because patriarchy's effect is global just as its system is global. And that's where our common interest lies. The call to sisterhood is bigger than just friendship. Forming bonds of friendship requires deliberate acts of choice, but sisterhood is built on a different code. The first code that sisterhood has to be built on is the clean slate factor. The clean slate factor is meant for how you reference your experiences with another woman (or girl) whom you feel may have done you wrong. This clean slate factor is another way of saying starting with a stance of forgiveness. Another of the primary codes of sisterhood is just common cordiality. Being cordial doesn't cost a thing, it avoids initial outward signs and acts of conflict or violence, and it promotes or underpins the respect necessary to work together to get things done, whether in a church setting where spiritual matters are tended to (Christian) or social, academic, or professional settings: society's playgrounds.

Sisterhood doesn't involve deliberate choice the way friendship does. And you inherit your family or marry into them, yet many natural sisters are not friends for various reasons. Sometimes there is a false perception that sisterhood requires no effort to have a close or cordial relationship. This is absolutely not true.

Having or being a sister in this new leadership of sisterhood involves a different kind of thought process and effort than friendship. Because of this false perception, that sisterhood takes no effort to maintain, sisterhood is taken lightly or taken for granted. Sisters can have a more casual relationship, but friends have a deeper intimacy that takes time to build. And friendships are given time, effort and nurturing necessary to build the best possible relationships. However, the truth is, given where patriarchy has placed us, it appears that more deliberate effort is required and necessary for sisterhood to grow and blossom. For it to evolve into a leadership as we transition from one state to a more better and needed state it's going to require specific work and commitment.

One of the most powerful actions between friends is listening, and it's often missing between natural sisters. I propose that there are at least three essential ingredients for successful development of sisterhood, just as in friendship. They are as follows:

- listening
- respect
- humility

But if you look further, there's also a fourth element in friendship that's not always part of relationships between sisters. It's acceptance. Listening, respect, humility, and acceptance are essential to friendship but usually absent from sisterhood.

Again, listening, respect, humility, and acceptance are missing from sisterhood because sisterhood and sisters are taken for granted. Their presence in our lives isn't a matter of choice. Under patriarchy, we were brainwashed into avoiding and opposing one another because we were forced into relationships with one another that we didn't choose. We resisted women we were compelled to share time and space with and never saw the benefit of sisterhood. This resistance has traveled with us throughout history and poisoned the way we treat women (other than our friends).

In any event, foehood isn't usually seen among a circle of friends unless something within the friendship circle goes awry. Therefore, it's easier to recognize among nonfriends. But that doesn't mean that listening, acceptance, respect, and humility aren't appropriate for our interactions with other women who don't happen to be in our circle. To be honest, they're quite essential.

A sister is a female sibling related by blood. But the term sister is also used to refer to women (and girls) who aren't related by blood yet treat each other with affection. When affection is expressed among women with a common interest who offer mutual support, it's referred to as sisterhood.

Sisterhood supports a kinship that honors the individuals within this hood of sisters based on unity, without the need for personal details. The call to sisterhood is a higher calling than friendship because foehood shows up more often among women and girls pursuing everyday activities where no intimacy is involved.

Foehood is most common among us; friendship ranks second. And until now, to many, a deliberate and genuine respect for the aspect of sisterhood wasn't seen as valuable, but it is! The idea of sisterhood inspires women to connect on a higher level because it honors respect, humility, acceptance, and listening—all common among friends.

The Image in the Mirror

A recent televised and social media news story reported that a popular celebrity's daughter was seen at a social event talking to a music mogul who's married. A picture of the two of them went viral online and in the media, along with opinionated and judgmental comments. Most of the negative comments about the woman suggested bad intentions toward this married man and were posted by other women.

This is another typical modern-day example of foehood. It presents itself as an innocent opinion but is often an act of brutal judgment and an attempt to question or even assassinate another woman's character.

Another recent news report cited the duchess of Wales and the princess of Wales and how they're constantly being compared against each other. Both men and women participate, but much of the gossip about who's more beautiful comes from other women.

Women in the music industry have to compete with one another for the same audience and livelihood. Current incidents involving some of these women reek of foehood and are prime examples of foehoodism.

Even if you're rich and famous, foehood can strike at any time, from anywhere. It happens among us every day, which is why it's time to view sisterhood from a different perspective. It's time to accept and understand why we've been living in the presence of our past for so long. It's time for us to understand that when we don't feel good about ourselves and when we feel threatened we act out of a foe-hood mind-set towards one another. (This foehood mind-set is applicable to both men and women; boys and girls). But it's time for us as women, as girls and as current and future leaders to act out against the system. Especially when the system celebrates, condones, or encourages our conflict. The system of patriarchy authored our conflict, contention, and intolerance of one another long ago. It's time for us to act out together against patriarchy through a new refined system of sisterhood.

The Leadership of Sisterhood

Sisterhood is not based on your culture or your race or your biology. We are sisters and have sisterhood because of our gender. We are women who share the same tears and disappointments, the same joys and successes. We share similar life experiences. And we deserve the chance to form a new sisterhood through leadership that secures it once and for all.

Every woman who's launched her own company or business, established her own earning power, and created her own wealth is a leader. She's improved the economy by providing jobs and increasing her community's tax base, besides advancing other women's economic stability and independence.

These women are leaders who dared to defy the traditional leadership model we inherited under patriarchy. They are the women and girls who rose up and said that business as usual does not allow us to serve our greater purpose and is therefore unacceptable.

Anytime you see a woman pastor who had the courage to establish her own church despite naysayers and perhaps her own fears, you're looking at a woman who rejected the old leadership model for pastoring. You're witnessing leadership built on a new and higher vision. It's an entrepreneurial model that seeks to start something new, something challenging, and something that might be scrutinized and criticized by those who appreciate only the status quo.

When a female employee decides to leave corporate America to pursue her own dream on her own terms, she enters into a new realm of leadership beyond the standard model. Her courage to step outside the box supports my opinion that leadership for women is always a pioneering venture. It involves more than the standard traditional model we were taught to follow.

To put an end to living unhealthily ever after, leadership for women must include the challenge of adding the sisterhood layer. This new territory is like the uncharted waters of entrepreneurship when we first entered them. When the professional and economic status quo for women failed to provide the necessary independence and stability, something had to give.

And now in that same way, we must usher in sisterhood, because the world's view of how we treat one another no longer works. Women must take the lead once again. We did it before, and we can and will do it again. I call this revival the leadership of sisterhood.

The leadership of sisterhood is a higher calling that demands change by us and for us. Yes, it's easier to make nice with our friends and to be cool with people we know. But the challenge of sisterhood is to be nice, cool, respectful, humble, caring, and kind to women we don't know and may not even like.

We can't be friends with everyone, but we can acknowledge a community of women with many common interests. These include respect, survival, and safety. We all want and need these things.

Our common interests are what make sisterhood the best option for creating a universal position founded on our precious experiences and stories. Some of our stories are universal, and some are unique, but all are worthy within the bonds of this community called sisterhood, whose code of conduct is respect, to be conveyed without fear of reprisal, judgment, or other foehoodism responses. If we choose this path, it will increase kindness and camaraderie and drastically reduce foehood experiences.

Under patriarchy, instructions in leadership were given to sons, not daughters. Daughters weren't expected to be anything more than role players in a one-sided scripted drama. Because all figures of power, ability, and authority were male, with the strong exception of Deborah (Lappidoth) (Barak)[5], Esther (Mordecai)[6], and Queen Vashti (Xerxes)[7], women had few role models for female leadership. The only choices available to women and girls in patriarchal family systems were preconceived roles acted out in rivalry and hostility.

Patriarchy created a catastrophe for women, and no one's going to fix it for us, so we have to fix it ourselves. But this is nothing new. We've started families, homes, businesses, careers, churches, nonprofits, and much more ourselves. Let's face it: as women, it's who we are and what we do.

It's our job and no one else's to make sisterhood a priority. We're the ones who must stop the humiliation and judgment of one another and offer one another respect and acceptance. The unity of women as sisters with common interests really is universal. So the language of sisterhood must also be universal if we're to put an end to foehoodism. Lisa Ross said, while making reference to Esther, God has a plan for our lives and we are given divine moments to alter

---

[5] Scholfield Holy Bible, King James Version, Judges 4:1-16

[6] Scholfiled Holy Bible, King James Version, Esther 4:4-16:

[7] Scholfield Holy Bible, King James Version, Esther 1: 9-22

circumstances. Therefore, we must stand with courage.[8] The leadership of sisterhood will take us, right now, seizing this divine moment to alter our current circumstances of foehood. The change will be the creation of a new circumstance. A circumstance of Sisterhood that we all need. We will face certain opposition however.

Our Challenge-Our Example-Our Strength: A Modern-Day Esther-Queen Vashti

Unfortunately, the first recorded woman to resist the values, beliefs and prominent pleasures of patriarchy is not celebrated as a leader. She is touted as disrespectful or disobedient to this system which wanted her to be paraded around before drunken men for their pleasure purposes only. No one asked her why she rejected the King, her husband's command to come and parade herself before a crowd of men who had been drinking for several days. It's only determined that her rejection of an order- to be objectified- was an act of insolence towards an accepted well established system. Not an act of protection for her own well-being. Not many have looked at Queen Vashti as a pioneering female leader who told the values and ways of patriarchy where to go. Her actions said I will not be used for my hips, lips, hair,

[8] Lisa Ross, "The Book of Esther-6 Powerful Lesson From the Bible" March 17, 2015, accessed July 17, 2019, https://www.crosswalk.com/Lisa Ross-inspirations.com

looks, and other attributes of femininity for the pleasures of others unless I choose to do so. Yet, the only story that is told surrounding her decision is a negative one or not told at all; negative or silence in the Church especially. The reason for this is that her story or voice behind her decision to "disobey" her husband and also patriarchy was not viewed as a leadership worthy designation or event. We must keep in mind that when there is a decision made that is not pleasing to nor appeasing of this system it's always going to be used against us to render us useless as leaders and useless to God. However, both women, Esther and Queen Vashti, decided to be used in a great way and both had the attitude of: if I have to risk my life to effect change in someone else's life I will. I will because this cause is bigger than me. Queen Vashti's actions represents a sister who had had enough of being compared, controlled and vilified because of her looks or failure to say yes, when a NO response is more appropriate to protect emotional health, mental health, and overall self-esteem. However, the fact that when she is spoken of or remembered it is in the context of disobedience speaks to the reality that there is a realm of society that really wants to maintain the status quo and keep silent about women's feelings about how patriarchy has caused her to feel or has devalued her choices and decisions when she does something different, but yet perhaps, Godly centered. This is the risk Queen Vashti was willing to take when she decided that living within the status quo would not work for her any more.

Like Esther, and Deborah Queen Vashti is important, too, as an example of female leadership because we must get over the fact that there will be some who looks at this call to sisterhood and any renunciations of the harmful DNA of our current mind-sets that we were historically conditioned to accept and respond with as extreme or disobedient or even disrespectful to "God" as well as to the set-up that has "worked" for years. These are all lies. The truth is that this IS NOT God's set-up and it really hasn't worked for years. It actually has eaten away at our core for years and turned us into created foes. However, here is how we can usher in a new solidarity:

1. First, *listen* to each other with understanding, empathy, and a willingness to accept one another for who we are.

2. Second, *stop* looking to the values and beliefs of patriarchy when we engage with one another. These values and beliefs only encourage comparison, insecurity, and jealousy among us. Choose to give other women the freedom to speak, even if their language isn't yours.

3. Third, *stop* thinking that foehood and its experiences don't exist just because you have close girlfriends. Foehood experiences don't happen between friends but between women who aren't friends. Without understanding this reality, we're missing valuable

opportunities to connect with other women and ex-change stories.

4. Fourth, *take responsibility* for bringing about the change that's needed. We must be brave and fear-less just like our entrepreneurial predecessors were.

5. Fifth, *accept* the fact that this new element of female leadership is sisterhood. We must abolish the foehood narratives that have dominated our consciousness for so long and renew our relationships.

6. Finally, *understand* that to replace foehood with sis-terhood, we have to believe that we're too strong and too wise to fail. It's worth doing the work that's re-quired because there's a real benefit when women (and girls) want to get along, whether or not we're friends.

We truly didn't know that patriarchy and its brainwashing were behind women's relationship struggles with one an-other. We believed the lie that said we couldn't get along, and hostile interactions between women were seen as the rule in society and not the exception. Foehood was the product of our brainwashing, but foehood doesn't have to be the end of our story.

Sticking our heads in the sand and ignoring our foehood experiences is no longer acceptable. All women and girls must take up the new leadership model that's required in these critical times. Until we rise up and teach our daughters (our girls) to reject the lies we were told about one another, we'll be stuck in the cycle of foehood experiences. The dominant actors in society have never encouraged true connection between us because that would have been to their disadvantage.

We need one another's sisterhood now more than ever. We need one another because this male-driven system called patriarchy has torn us apart in so many ways and left us hurting one another. And the only reason is this: we didn't know we were under the control of a system set up to destroy our confidence, our trust in each other, and every ounce of loyalty and support between us.

The cure for everything that's been ailing us is to restore what patriarchy took away: sisterhood. So let's get on with this new form of leadership, the leadership of sisterhood.

Reader's Guide

1. Is a sisterhood movement needed at this time in society? Why? Why not?
2. Have you ever wondered why relationships between women (and girls) seem to be strained?
3. What are some of the negative stories you heard about women (and girls) when you were a child? A teenager? An adult?
4. Did you have any experiences that matched these negative stories?
5. What are some of your positive stories about your good girlfriends? What are the dynamics of these relationships? What has kept them together?
6. Have you ever thought about history's impact on present-day female relationships?
7. Have you ever considered or thought about how history has shaped women's (and girls') attitudes about themselves, their families, and others? What were your thoughts?

8. Is it safe to say that change is needed among us women (and girls)? If so, what kind of change?
9. What are some best practices we can develop for sisterhood?
10. What are some best practices for sisterhood that can reshape our overall attitudes toward one another?
11. Are our values, beliefs, and actions toward one another influenced by past generations? Our grandmothers? Mothers? Sisters? Friends? Are they influenced by our experiences?
12. What are our next steps for taking the lead in this sisterhood movement?
13. Knowing the origin of the problem, how difficult will it be to forgive a friend? A woman (or girl) who is not a friend? Why?
14. Can you be willing to agree to disagree and travel in the same circles at the same time without encouraging or participating in a foehood experience? Yes or no, please explain or discuss.

About the Author

Female leadership development has always been the passion and extended business of Dr. Fulton-Taylor. Whether serving in a leadership capacity in an established church organization, where she has been vastly and prolifically instrumental in their women's department, or whether operating her own nonprofit organizational program, Rehabilitation from the Inside Out, for women and girls in the Philadelphia Prison Systems (PPS), Riverside Correctional Facility (RCF), empowering women and girls to understand their value and worth outside of their histories and circumstances has always been in the forefront of every extended professional and academic decision. It was while on these dual and converging journeys through Christendom and social as well as correctional organizations that Dr. Fulton-Taylor discovered the connection between foehood (which is a word she has developed and defined) and patriarchy. Dr. Fulton-Taylor discovered that patriarchy had an effect on the female mind-set, value systems, and personal attitudes and beliefs that women and girls had about one another. Dr. Fulton-Taylor also discovered that these values, mind-sets, and personal attitudes were an extension of the male dominant point of view held about women and taught through conditioning and controlled circumstances, which were adapted to by women (and girls) as a means of survival. These adversarial survival skills were borne out of desperation or perceived loss of control, not initially as a matter of absolute choice. At these discoveries, Dr. Fulton-Taylor's research revealed that no one has ever, in this fashion, tied in or linked the current and modern-day systemic problems commonly talked about as existing between women and girls to history, biblical antiquity, or the establishment of patriarchy. As a result, Dr. Fulton-Taylor identified the problem, examined its origin, and has now unleashed an opportunity for change and an initial blueprint to start from. This unleashing, which Dr. Fulton-Taylor has labeled as the "leadership of sisterhood," is wrapped in an unattended-to area of sisterhood, which requires a new layer to female leadership. This sisterhood, as unveiled through research observation and personal experience, has been redefined as a hood of not biologically related women (and girls) with common connections that require, demand, and are underpinned by respect, acceptance, forgiveness, and humility. *From Foehood to Sisterhood* was conceived on the journeys that Dr. Fulton-Taylor traveled. It grew in the loins of her doctoral work and completion (2017) and is now birthed through the authorship of this book, which is her first of many as she unlocks and brings to the forefront the required understanding of the attitude, mind-set, thinking, and consciousness of foehood and how it has infiltrated all relationship dynamics by creating, fostering, and promoting conflict. The first step is to name foehood—the byproduct of patriarchy, as the reason for sisterhood breakdown. The second steps is to address the breakdown through an approach principled in social as well as biblical strategies and insight.

Glossary

foehood: False or perverted version of sisterhood (or brotherhood) where destructive rivalry and angrily expressed opposition toward one another is apparent or displayed or expressed through one's actions or deeds against another or between two or more persons.

foehoodism: The practice of foehood.

leadership of sisterhood: Groundbreaking, pioneering, fearless, confident approach toward initiating and facilitating change within female interactions and relationships through deliberate implementation of mutual support of women (and girls), using tools of listening, accepting, respecting, and humility, in order to renounce all and any negative attitudes, beliefs, or dispositions toward other women (and girls).

spiritual entrepreneur (or spritualpreneur): Someone who creates their (her) own platform for sharing their (her) spirituality with others; a (female) person with spiritual and religious beliefs and convictions who establishes their (her) own church, religious organization, or program using nontraditional gender-defining or demeaning limitations.

Acknowledgments

First, I would like to thank God, who gave me this great task and entrusted His revelation concerning his queens, princesses, duchesses, and leaders with me. Secondly, I want to thank my husband for always encouraging me, believing in my life's purpose, and never allowing me to give up on myself or to live in the dark places of my discouragement. Thirdly, my mommy, who taught me to exist in the moment, never stop being myself, and that what is for me is for me; I didn't always believe it, but I trusted what she said, and now I can finally see what she meant. Because of my faithful mother, I too am faithful. Because of my confident mother, I now walk in confidence. She pulled me from the depths of purpose despair, when I thought what I had was insignificant and unimportant to anyone but me. She said, "God has given you this revelation, and He will bring it into the open." Thanks, Mom.

To my readers, thank you for your time and attention to the message and being honest. To my editor, my sister from another mister, thank you for making me focus on plain language and sticking with me from the doctoral thesis to this book. For every experience that I have encountered, I am grateful, because without the experiences, there would be no insight. And last but not least, thank you, Bishop, for encouraging me through all my arduous processes. It was not easy, I am sure, but you have blessed me in ways that words will never express. Because you didn't Die In the Winter, the Sisterhood season has come!

Sisterhood Best Practices

1._____

2. _____

3. _____

4._____

5._____

6._____

7._____

8._____

9._____

10._____

Bibliography

Covey, Stephen R. *7 Habits of Highly Successful People.* New York: Free Press, 1989.

Fox, Christina. "When We Try to Put New Wine into Old Wineskins." January 14, 2015.

Fulton, Eloise M. "The Impact of Patriarchy on Female Leadership in the Church." Doctoral thesis, Lutheran Theological Seminary at Philadelphia, 2016.

Hickey, Marilyn. *Breaking Generational Curses: Overcoming the Legacy of Sin in Your Family.* Tulsa, OK: Harrison House Publishing, 2000.

Keneally, Meghan. "Police Investigating Alleged Bullying in 9 Year Old Girl's Apparent Suicide." December 11, 2018.

Ross, Lisa, "The Book of Esther-6 Powerful Lessons from the Bible." March 17, 2015

Scholfield Holy Bible, King James Version. http://www. Biblegateway.com.

www.ingramcontent.com/pod-product-compliance
Lightning Source LLC
Chambersburg PA
CBHW050400290526
45786CB00003B/1068

* 9 7 8 1 4 8 0 8 8 0 1 9 1 *